# MACERATION
## JAY KOPHY

This is a work of fiction. All names, characters, places, and incidents are a product of the author's imagination. Any resemblance to real events or persons, living or dead, is entirely coincidental.

Published by Akashic Books
©2023 Jay Kophy
ISBN: 978-1-63614-128-2

All rights reserved
Printed in China
First printing

Akashic Books
Brooklyn, New York
Instagram, Twitter, Facebook: AkashicBooks
E-mail: info@akashicbooks.com
Website: www.akashicbooks.com

African Poetry Book Fund
*Prairie Schooner*
University of Nebraska
110 Andrews Hall
Lincoln, Nebraska 68588

## TABLE OF CONTENTS

*Preface by Therí Alyce Pickens* 5

The Lake Disappears at the Mouth of the River 9
Ghanaian Arithmetic 10
What You Will Hear When You Dip Your Head into the Volta Lake 12
Pharmakeia 14
Fuck Your Lecture on Patience My People Are Dying 16
Hagiography 17
Baptism 19
Is There Another Way We Can Drown without Dying 20
Invocation 22
The Disappearance of God 23
Memory Is a Parable 24
It Begins with Love 25
Heaven Is a Parable 26
Atrophy 28
Returning 29
Taxonomy 30
History Is a Parable 32

*Notes 34*
*Acknowledgments 35*

# PREFACE
*by Therí Alyce Pickens*

Maceration is an extraction process in which what is soaked disintegrates because of its prolonged exposure to liquid. What of macerated flesh or lands?

Jay Kophy's *Maceration* locates this inquiry mostly in the geopolitical space of Ghana, often referencing Lake Volta. He opens the collection with "welcome me home in a language / that is of my blood," an invitation that is as startling as it is heartbreaking. The imperative here suggests that the speaker is already an outsider, begging to be let back in, to return. And, yet, return, as the rest of the poem intimates, is impossible. Throughout the collection, each speaker—beautifully, lovingly, painstakingly—negotiates their status as outsider while also understanding themselves as inextricably linked to and made by the spaces referenced. For those of us who have felt homeless, whether by fiat or fiasco (often synonymous), this collection feels like opening our journals, our most primal screams.

*Maceration*, as a collection, is shaped by loss and memory, even as it questions how each of these experiences come into being. As with any process of extraction and disintegration, the poetic engine behind *Maceration* is the movement of liquid, usually water. In moments when the water comes—floods, blood, drowning—it is overwhelming, violent, even in its expression of might and awesome power. Lake Volta functions as a specific touchstone allowing both the title and the images to speak to water's power to destroy, to macerate flesh, to extract essence and feeling.

When water is absent (droughts, thirst) it remains a constant pressure, exerting itself on people, places, and memory. In Kophy's poems, the drought or the memory of rain (precisely because it has not come) becomes another way of thinking about drowning and fatigue. Many of the speakers continue to yearn for water that is destructive, even as they know it is so.

One of the most compelling poems in the collection is "Fuck Your Lecture on Patience My People Are Dying." Regardless of the expletive or perhaps because of it, this poem captures the core of this collection: the beauty and the horror of water, meditations on the limits of language, and cyclical natures of destruction and, of course, that tenacious and most torturous of feelings, hope.

Hope and pain are tricksters. Each has a warping effect on one's perception of the present. While pain sometimes feels more real than hope, hope too can be a powerful inclination. In Kophy's work, the two are not decidedly cleaved from each other.

And yet, it is difficult to discuss hope without invoking the maudlin. Kophy's poems capture the subtlety of hope. It is in the prayers and the laughter that trill across several poems. It is in Kophy's use of imagination and the imagination described by Kophy's speakers. Within the embrace or rejection of metaphors, the poems communicate a desire for better. Hope, it seems, is liquid: taking the shape of whatever vessel contains it regardless of shape, size, or whether it has feathers.

Kophy's emphasis on religion becomes instructive. Much of this collection questions the narratives we have come to associate with faith. That is to say, Kophy considers what happens when we pray, what happens when we seek to be generous without resources, and how rituals like baptism perform as metaphors. In one poem, "Invocation," the speaker seems to whisper "but sometimes you wake from a nightmare / to find your hands shaking from carrying / the wounded memories you've swallowed." The gerunds keep us in the present. The shaking happens now; the carrying happens now. The threat of nightmarish memories is currently upon us even if, as the poem itself avers, waking from nightmares is a "sometimes" occurrence. The collection as a whole engages in slightly skeptical conversation with faith, noting in "The Disappearance of God" that every new story is a resurrection of sorts.

In reading Kophy's work, I cannot help but think of geographies, in addition to Ghana, where those of us who are rootless but returning, pained but hopeful, fearful and faithful see the effects of water (or its lack) on the land and the people. This collection is elastic enough to stretch to places where access to water determines life itself. *Maceration* is both a meticulous chronicling of survival and a critique of the conditions in which one is forced to survive.

I travel through these poems at a slow ambling pace. *Maceration* takes its time, soaks into the skin. By the time you finish, you may find yourself changed by the essence of what has been extracted, summed up in the last two lines:

> and this is how I choose to end this story
> by saying, *I love you*, in this language which isn't ours.

# THE LAKE DISAPPEARS AT THE MOUTH OF THE RIVER

welcome me home in a language
that is of my blood. that reminds me
of the delight of children at the shore
of a lake that was once their farm.

when I am home, I know the birds
sing to the earth from the sky
for reinstatement of the things lost.

yet the names of the dead trees
in the Volta Lake cannot return
to my people. and my people cannot
return to their history without
first drowning. this is to say

in this country, everything we know
dissolves at the edge of the lake
making remembrance an act of resurrection.

but there is no miracle if the messiah too has drowned.

on an early saturday morning, a mother
heavies a bucket with the same water
she knows cleaned off the stains on her baby's skin

and maybe

    this is how love begins.

## GHANAIAN ARITHMETIC
*after Natalie Diaz*


in Ghana, about 38% of the population
do not have access to potable water
but hundreds die of drowning in Accra
annually when the floods come
and when the floods come, they remind us of
the difference between empty and emptied.

what is the place of memory in the shaping of identity?

I can only remember the sound of rainwater
as an invitation to leave washable footprints on the earth
I cannot forget the sound of rainwater so heavy
it is believed to be an invocation of a flood.

but sometimes flood means pour
which implies offering—giving something
holy through a ritual. meaning something
was sacrificed.

it's been 38 years since the drought
but people are still thirsty
it was 18 years before the drought
when the government flooded part of the Volta River Basin
forcing about 1% of the population to relocate
with their memories but not the trees.

we are Ghanaians
so we do not care about the trees

but we are filled up in church trying
to pray away the hunger.

but sometimes hunger means desire,
means to be wanted. to be taken. to be
swallowed whole without leaving much
for remembrance even when a name is invoked.

in 2018, about 0.6% of Ghanaians drowned.
in my language the word for *drown* translates to *water has collected*
which sounds like a prayer of return for what water has always owned
sounds more acceptance than sorrow
more desire than grief
and this is how maceration begins.

## WHAT YOU WILL HEAR WHEN YOU DIP YOUR HEAD INTO THE VOLTA LAKE

the unrest of the land where my people planted seeds
and harvested themselves

sitting beneath a water they cannot forgive.

the roots and stems standing in the water calling out
to trees to remind them of who they are.

the lake singing about how no one drowns anymore
because everyone has learned how to breathe underwater.

the promise God made to my people never to destroy
their homes with water again.

the ghosts of those whose farms were destroyed by the water
saying *look, starvation is the only meaning for lake
and there's no error in calling every puddle of water flood.*

here, let me help you understand.

*yesterday
we drank the flood we collected in our hands
to quiet the hunger in our stomach.*

*today
we are no different from the flood that taught us
that to survive is to be solvent—
to eat without the burden of satisfaction.*

*tomorrow*

*we will wash our face with the flood that swallowed our voice
to remember and remember and remember to forget*

*that home is a verb.*

## PHARMAKEIA

in my hometown, here's how you cure hunger.

first, stretch out your arms and collect
your name with your clenched fist.

then pour it into a pot that is being heated
by the anger of the sun.

wait for 15 minutes

and add a little bit of the water sitting
in your empty hands and stir.

you may feel a little sting in your eyes
when the steam rises and meets them.

when that happens, you may use your mother tongue
to express your anger or frustration or whatever is
unclean enough to be dressed in English.

*but English is what is unclean* is what I can say to the sky.

shhh
don't talk while you cook
like you don't while your father speaks
even when he's speaking in his sleep.

now crush cubes of laughter and sprinkle that
over it. it may start to smell like a miracle

but don't be deceived. over here a miracle isn't
a miracle until it's done in the name of the government.

shhh
now add salt and stir till you can hear your grandma's
voice telling you to pray for a soft rain that cannot flood your home.

wait for 5 minutes

then pour and hold it in your mouth till it tastes
similar to blood

                and finally

                            swallow.

## FUCK YOUR LECTURE ON PATIENCE MY PEOPLE ARE DYING
*After Noor Hindi*

and to this day I can't write about the joy of rain
without remembering those who became water bodies
as their names became memories.
all my memories of water are graveyards.
in this country, all the graves are empty
because the dead are trying to make a better place
before our arrival. this is not a metaphor.
we do not believe in metaphors but we believe in ghosts
only when they were born from someone who died from drowning
or hunger, or whatever translates a body into an empty sky.
into an empty sky, a tired man shouts *here, we die even before we are born*
and I swear this is also not a metaphor.
so ask this, what is the relationship between power and blood?
in Jerusalem, Jesus said to give what belongs to Caesar to Caesar.
in Ghana, we give what we have to those who don't have us.
I know I'm Ghanaian when I beat misery into laughter
trying to make a crown out of thorns of grief.
how long do we have to wait to stop burying ourselves before we die?
how do we have to wait before we die?
how have we died?

## HAGIOGRAPHY

*Bring me*
*to where*
*my blood runs*
—Wanda Coleman

    a half-baked body lying quietly on the ground
    becomes evidence of the punishment of resistance.
    and we watch this still body, intently, as though it will
    react to us making a memory of it.

    we don't mind the stench. we are used to death now.
    for what has history taught us
    if not the many ways to rename blood
    to replace loss with sacrifice.

    the price for this death is understanding.
    look at what you have made us into.
    even God, for a moment, questioned the purpose of blood
    streaming out of a body when His son died.
    but maybe this is because He isn't from here
    He isn't used to the stench of what He loves rotting in his hands
    to say their name and taste absence instead of home.

    this home is a religion of hunger and dissolution
    every day we wake up is a disobedience of the daily ritual.

    hallelujah!
    another messiah has been found lying quietly on the belly
    of the earth, limbs arranged like he's resting on a cross
    with a placard in his hands saying

*in my father's house are many mansions
and I am going to prepare a place for you.*

and his body said blood instead of amen.

## BAPTISM

over here
we do not laugh when the rains come.

we do not build altars of songs
thanking God for the water
and all the nourishment that comes with it.

we do not dip our hands in the water
asking to be forgiven for what we did in the drought.

instead
        we speak silence
                far better than the dead

for being reminded of what we want to forget.
what we want to forget is what remembers us.

and we do not want to remember us.
we do not want to remember

until the water
pushes back into our mouths what we bury

in the holes between the teeth of the earth
with a lifeless body as reference saying

*nothing can be hidden in water for long*
*and this flood is evidence of that.*

# IS THERE ANOTHER WAY WE CAN DROWN WITHOUT DYING

which is to ask if it is possible to paint a boy without
pouring water into his wounded hands

without giving a voice back to the ghosts he has starved
with silence.

my father is a man of many portraits

each picture reminds me of the story of a boy
who covers his feet with sand to feel at home when the rains come
who carries water in his hands like it is fire
afraid to drink the same thing that turned his brother's body lifeless.

did you know that even blood is another name for enraged water?

every night
in a short prayer
my father calls the Volta Lake a soldier, a predator, a disease.

he calls it anything that kills instead of its name

and this is how I know the Lake has turned all his grief
into the color of water.

what is the cost of mourning those who were sacrificed
for the cleansing of sins?

in my hometown
we bear the harshness of the sun
by throwing all our anger into the Volta Lake

yet we curse her
for swallowing our bodies in retaliation.

## INVOCATION

the rains cannot wash away the ache
that is buried in the muscles of the body.
so you burn incense to cleanse whatever
grief has made a home of
to make holy a vessel molded from dirt.

love songs are made of this
hymns of heartbreak and dirges.
grief is an expense of living
and myths are created from the laughter
that waits in between.
this way time becomes a synonym for faith
like the earth revolving around what it loves.
as if to say
language is a repetition of movement
a ritual of tomorrows performed today
an act of naming something to reach its tenderness.

but sometimes you wake from a nightmare
to find your hands shaking from carrying
the wounded memories you've swallowed
so you say a short prayer
to the sky because the night is taking too long.

# THE DISAPPEARANCE OF GOD

at twilight
just before the sun dies at the edge of the city
I see birds travel in a straight line
then fade by permeating a cloud
and emerge from another opening
like a thread going through a piece of cloth to make a stitch

which reminds me of my mother's old butterfly sewing machine
singing its way back to her through a torn shirt
like an echo navigating its way home through history and memory.

my earliest childhood memory
of going to school begins with blood.
wait, not with blood but with sweat making a map of my forehead
not with sweat but with tears streaming into my wailing mouth.
this is the burden of memory
too much wanting can leak into it.
and for years I have carefully tended every bit of it
trying to preserve every moment.

but sometimes in my reckless desire for evocation
imagination speaks into what I try to remember
turns the roots of a story into a new beginning
making a metaphor of what already exists
which means whatever is known wanes and dies.

but at the end is a resurrection, a new creation.
and this too is a miracle.
amen.

## MEMORY IS A PARABLE

even the birds know the sky
is nothing but another door.

I watch them disappear through it
and wonder if this is what language
does to memory.

what we do to remember
is where we go to disappear.

sometimes I run to the Lake for help
but this water also cannot save me.

## IT BEGINS WITH LOVE
*After Romeo Oriogun*

somewhere on the vastness of the Volta Lake, a child is cleaning the surface of the water with his hands before casting his net into the quiet water as if to see how it begins its day. child, the water begins with love, with a promise of newness, with a sigh of satisfaction, with everything we pray for when we want to return home. and this is how hunger besets us. makes of us the offspring of a lost home. it begins with love, I tell you, it always begins with love, even this hunger of trafficked children wanting to be renamed by their mothers. to one day return smelling less like the water. but instead, we see their bodies come back to us asking for a worthy burial. it always begins with love, I tell you, even drowning. how the water takes us in whole, without restraint, willing to give us itself until we are soft again. what is the cost of history to the desire for movement? in the loneliness of a city where language bears no resemblance to memory, a bloated body is evidence of yesterday's rain and I am the stranger asking to be welcomed with a handful of water to clean my hands.

## HEAVEN IS A PARABLE

in Accra, the good die from hunger or drowning
or whatever survival reincarnates into
before they are born

and the angels have sold their wings and halos
but we still pretend to be angels

and no one is late because time doesn't exist here
which means we don't die

and me, my brothers, sisters, mothers, and fathers
can't afford most of the houses but these empty
apartments add a lot of color to the city

and all the first-borns are second parents.
but we laugh and laugh and still laugh
because that too is a form of prayer
a blessing to whoever is close enough to hear it.

and even though God doesn't live here anymore
we still shout his names in church, in peril, in bed

and we don't get tired of mentioning names
because we carry a lot of history on our tongues

and yes, history has been unkind to us
but we laugh and laugh and still laugh
because that is too is a type of mask
a blessing to those who don't want to treat what is wounded.

like how

the pearly gates have surrendered to rust
but we are waiting for God to come fix them.

# ATROPHY

I don't remember the names of a lot of things.
anything you name becomes your possession.
sometimes I look in the mirror and forget who I am.
yes, memory is a joke.

as a child, I swallowed too much English.
now I've become tired of knocking on the door
of a house where blood can mean stranger and family
at the same time.

but sometimes this lake is evidence
that home is not a place but the arrival
a reminder that language is the only way we get to be home.
yet I have always been frightened
when I realize my Ewe is too malnourished to survive
outside my mouth.

sometimes I tend to confuse listening for understanding.
is the mouth the safest place to hide secrets
when its function is to translate the body into sound?

I have come to believe that whatever is dipped
into a new home becomes born again. praise the Lord.

in my language, when someone says they are going home
they mean blood is going back to blood.

## RETURNING

in a conversation with my mother about my hometown
she says blood has nothing to do with belonging
which is to say we do not come from a people or place but from naming
and what is naming if not a prayer
where every word is a reflection carrying more than one face
like how the word *etsi* means water and to grow
as if to say anything expandable carries an attribute of water.

there are some forms of water I am still not conversant with.
for instance, I am too familiar with rain
but winter is a stranger to me.
which is to say memory is tethered to language
which is to say language always returns me
back where my body cannot be present
to make alive again a place where everything is meant to drown
like the Volta Lake where dead cocoa stems
are the only memories the water cannot swallow.

this story doesn't change but the language to it does
like memory eating its way into history.
every historical statement is a journey to a place of recognition
that may or may not exist.
as in, history is a translation. it is what sits
between a name and its understanding.

## TAXONOMY
*After Chris Abani*

name it abode
name it the doorway to memory
name it *Torman* instead of Tema
when the sea is singing.
name it the home of wanderers
                              say the land of calabash
                              where the waters split rock.
                              name it in honor of arrival
                              a new beginning, a resurrection.
                              hallelujah! the messiah is here.

name it satisfaction
    name it reclamation
                say *kormi* not cornmeal.
name it morning ritual
    name it the offering and sacrifice
                      of our fathers, their names growing
                            out of the earth to fill our empty mouths
name it identity, we are what we eat
    name it *nududu*
                which means hunger doesn't live here
                      which means rebirth, which means prayer.

name it rebellion
    name it *sagrenti war*
    name it a battle cry
say the ocean will carry us home.
    name it the inheritance of kings

    name it kingdom
    name it the city of God
say the land is this body.
    do not say history is written by the conquerors.
    name it as heavy as blood sinking into the earth
the end of an old life, the start of a new story.

                      name it forgetful
                name it *ayigbe*
              name it mystifying
        name it a synonym for refusal
    for all the memories that couldn't
        be collected in your hands.
              name it the price of migration
                    say your people instead of my people
                        say this language is not mine
                            say nothing, then say *I*.

## HISTORY IS A PARABLE

and this is how I was taught to begin every story
like a voyage, a ritual, a resurrection
the rising of a changeless sun giving the day a new name.

this way it can be said that history is only as divine as the malleability of iron
which is susceptible to rust because of its need to undo its starvation for time.

and what is the value of a thing, if not a hunger for its history?
a reminder to build altars for the things I cannot forget
like the first time someone called me *ayigbe*
even though he didn't understand what it meant.

and what that meant was that in Accra my language is still a stranger
sitting at the edge of the city waiting for me to take it home.

and I don't know much about my hometown
except that it was named after a lake that spared my people from thirst
and was undone by another lake which shares no language with them

as if to say that any language which swallows the history of others is
    without love.

I've always imagined language as an element of love
how it moves from one person to another as an expression of faith
in search of understanding even if it's not there

but you are always here, or should I say here is always you.
which is something we attribute to the things we remember
even though they may not necessarily be ours.

and this is how I choose to end this story
by saying, *I love you*, in this language which isn't ours.

## NOTES

The significance of naming and names, for identity, memory, and remembrance, is imprinted in the culture of almost every tribe in Ghana. However, some very popular names of places, food, events, and people existing today in their current form are born from the corruption of their sounds. "Taxonomy" attempts to explore the emergence and cause of the corruption of these names.

## ACKNOWLEDGMENTS

My thanks to the editors of the following journals and anthologies in which these poems, sometimes in different forms or with different titles, first appeared:

*Lolwe*: "History Is a Parable" and "Returning"
*Indianapolis Review*: "Echo"
*A Voice Is a Voice: The Resistance Issue*: "Fuck Your Lecture on Patience My People Are Dying"
*Rogue Agent Journal*: "Hagiography"
"Pharmakeia" and "What You Will Hear When You Dip Your Head into the Volta Lake" were selected as the winning submissions of the 2020 Samira Bawumia Literature Prize and published in its anthology.